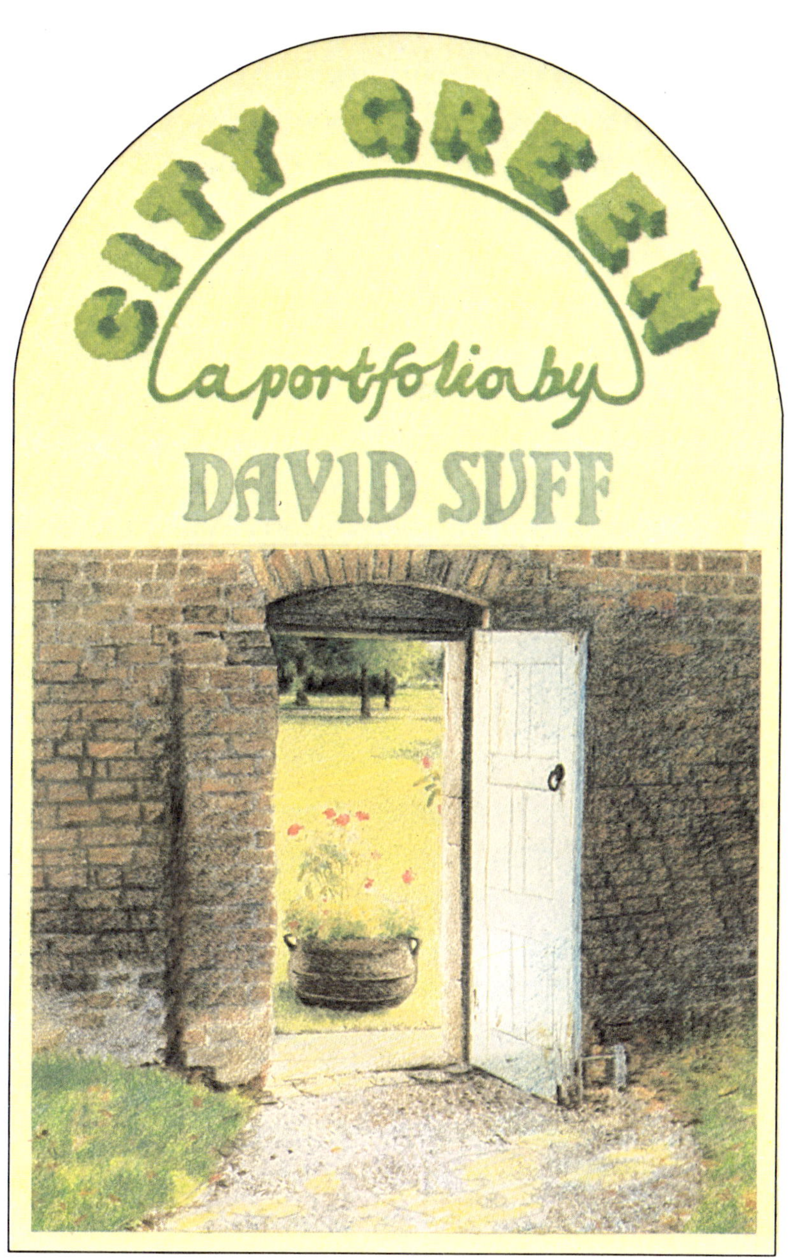

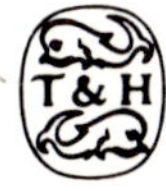

Thames and Hudson

First published in the United States by Thames and Hudson Inc., 500 Fifth Avenue, New York, New York 10110

Library of Congress Catalog Card Number 83-50525
ISBN 0-500-23386-1

Printed in Spain

INTRODUCTION

A childhood in Scotland and Malta is a good beginning for any young artist fascinated by gardens and plants of all kinds.

My very first memories, hazy now, of the rich lush greenery in Devon where I was born were soon overlaid with the misty colours of northern Britain and the dry Mediterranean landscapes of the Maltese coast.

The result is a kind of interior garden, luminous and intensely mysterious, which lies behind every one of my paintings. It's not only a visual image, but an atmosphere, an emotional response to a scene or view.

When I came to London to study at the Royal College of Art, I was astonished to find so many secret and not-so-secret gardens flourishing in every district, after surviving the most amazing onslaughts of destruction and construction. Armed with a bus ticket, a map, and sketching materials, I have set out time and time again to find one, only to discover three or four.

When I start to work, the sketches come first, in pencil or coloured crayons, watercolours or pen and ink. Every view is different; the weather is important and affects the medium I use – a garden in the rain is a very special place, but watercolours will run into a messy blurred wash. Very cold weather means stiff fingers and hard wax, so charcoal or a soft pencil will be best. Occasionally I will take a copper etching-plate with me, and draw tentatively on to the plate itself. Much of my work is made on these plates because I love the mysterious shadows which the tiny black lines add to the colours. They seem to add a dream-like quality, a sense of time past and time remembered, of long-forgotten summers and distant autumn winds.

All this I want to say in a few square inches, so the choice of place and image becomes absolutely vital. I will often take photographs in addition to making sketches and colour notes, taking scraps of real flowers and shrubs for colour and shape, recording a dozen different views of the same object. Sometimes I go back in different weather conditions; sometimes I want to keep the image clear and distinct as I first saw it. Eventually I decide on my approach, and then it is back to the studio to begin the process of transforming what is in my mind on to the paper.

With an etching, a wax ground is laid on to a copper plate, and the image is drawn with a special tool, cutting through the wax to the soft metal underneath. The drawing must be done in reverse, like all printing processes, before being dipped into an acid bath which etches into the copper along the lines where the wax has been removed. This action is described as 'biting', and when the lines are deep enough, the plate is taken out of the acid and the wax cleaned off with turpentine, leaving the plate ready for the ink. Copper needs a little warming to help the oil-based ink flow evenly. A rag carefully rubbed over the plate ensures that ink will lie evenly in the acid-etched lines; and the remaining ink is then cleaned off the rest of the surface. Finally, the printing itself is done in a press, with dampened paper laid over the plate. As the press is turned by hand, the ink in the lines is forced into the paper, and prints the image. The damp etching is removed and put between sheets of blotting-paper to dry under a weight. It will be three or four days before the etching is ready to be hand-coloured.

The etching process seems lengthy compared to a simple drawing or painting, but it has many advantages. First, a number of prints can be made of the same view, and until the lines begin to wear down, each will be sharp and clear. It is also possible to change the appearance of a scene with additional details of slanted rain or snow-flakes.

Sometimes, of course, the garden itself dictates the approach; formal paving with brightly coloured beds can look lighter and more brilliant with watercolour or acrylic paints.

Tiny paved islands full of pots of flowers, rolling acres of grass, cultivated allotments and wild, weed-sown tangles – nowhere is very far from a patch of green, if only we have the time and patience to look. With these etchings and paintings of a few favourite places, I hope to encourage others to look for and enjoy a glimpse of natural life in the most urban part of any town – and most of all, to learn to see their surroundings with a fresh eye.

David Suff

David Suff studied at the Royal College of Art, and his work has appeared in Royal Academy shows, in exhibitions held by the Royal Society of Etchers and Engravers, the National Society of Etchers, Painters and Engravers and in one-man exhibitions.

His prints appear regularly in Christie's Contemporary Art Society, and in 1981 he published Knot Fire, *a book of poetry. He also lectures and works as an etching technician. David Suff lives with his wife and daughter in London.*

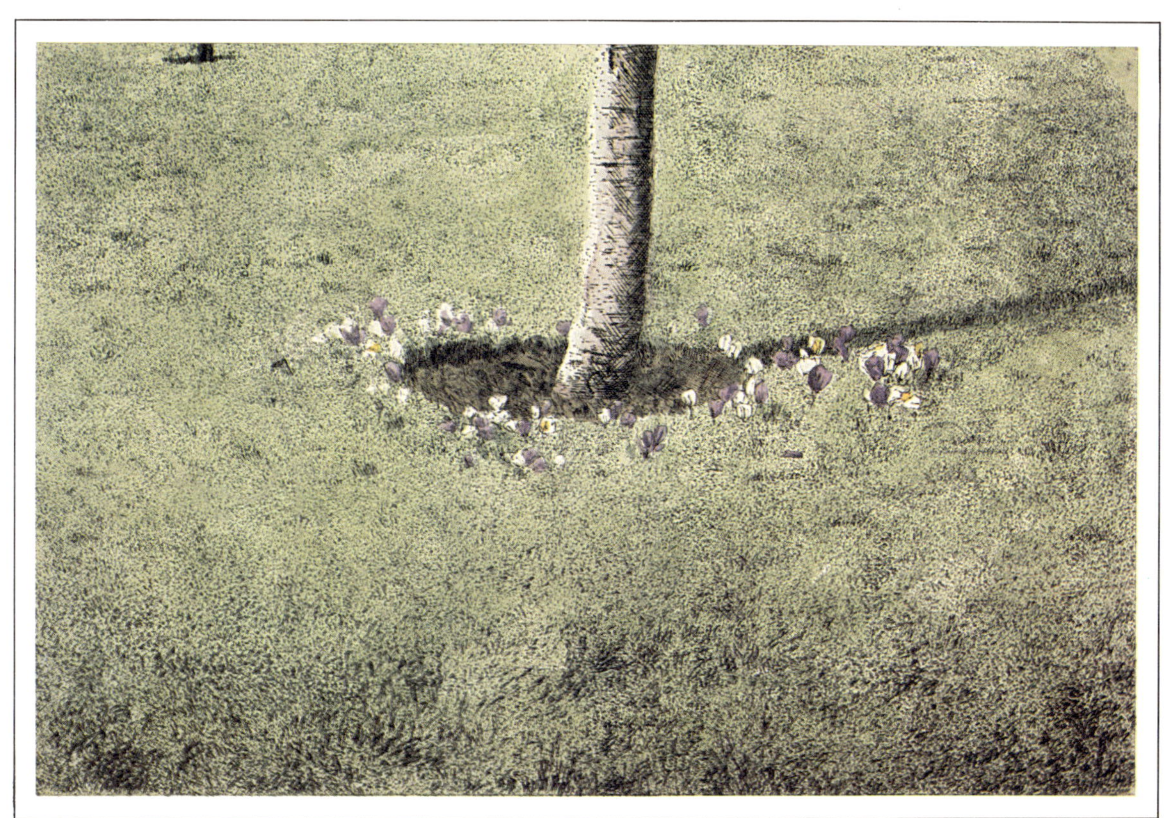

Crocus circle ~ Spring in Green Park

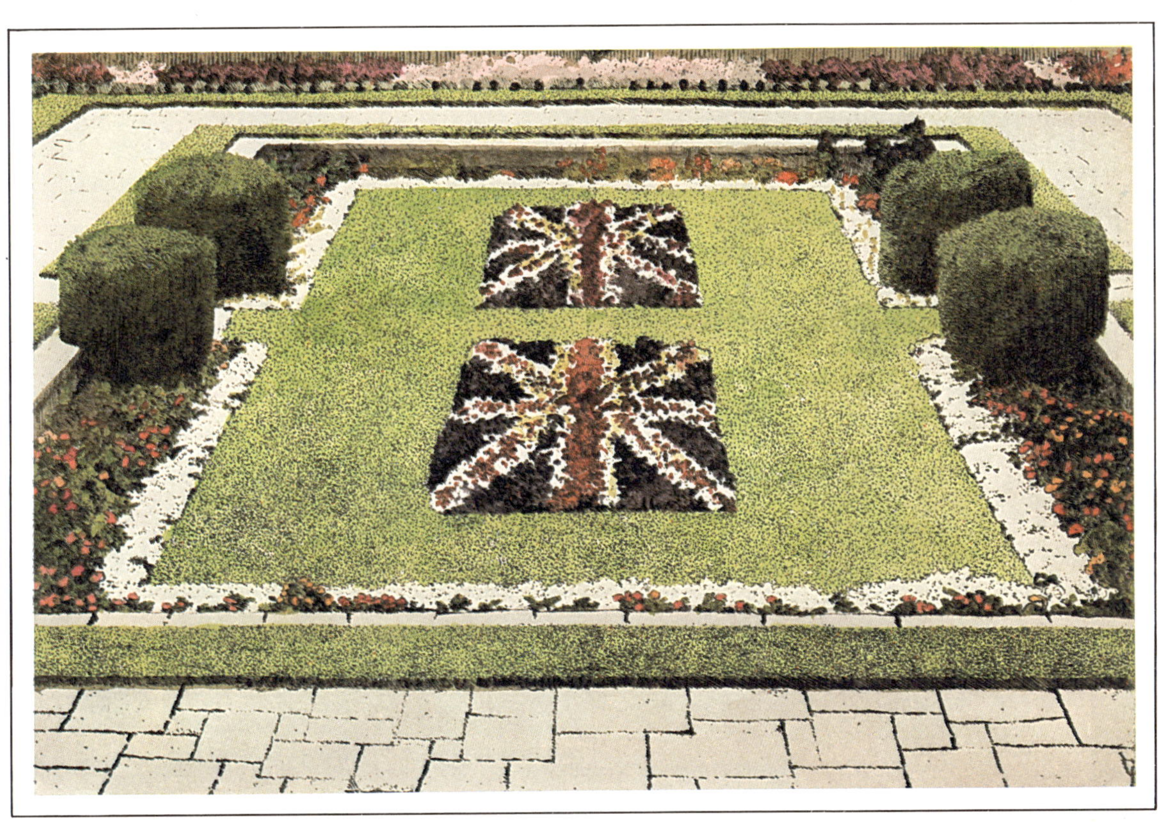

Union Jack, Horniman Gardens

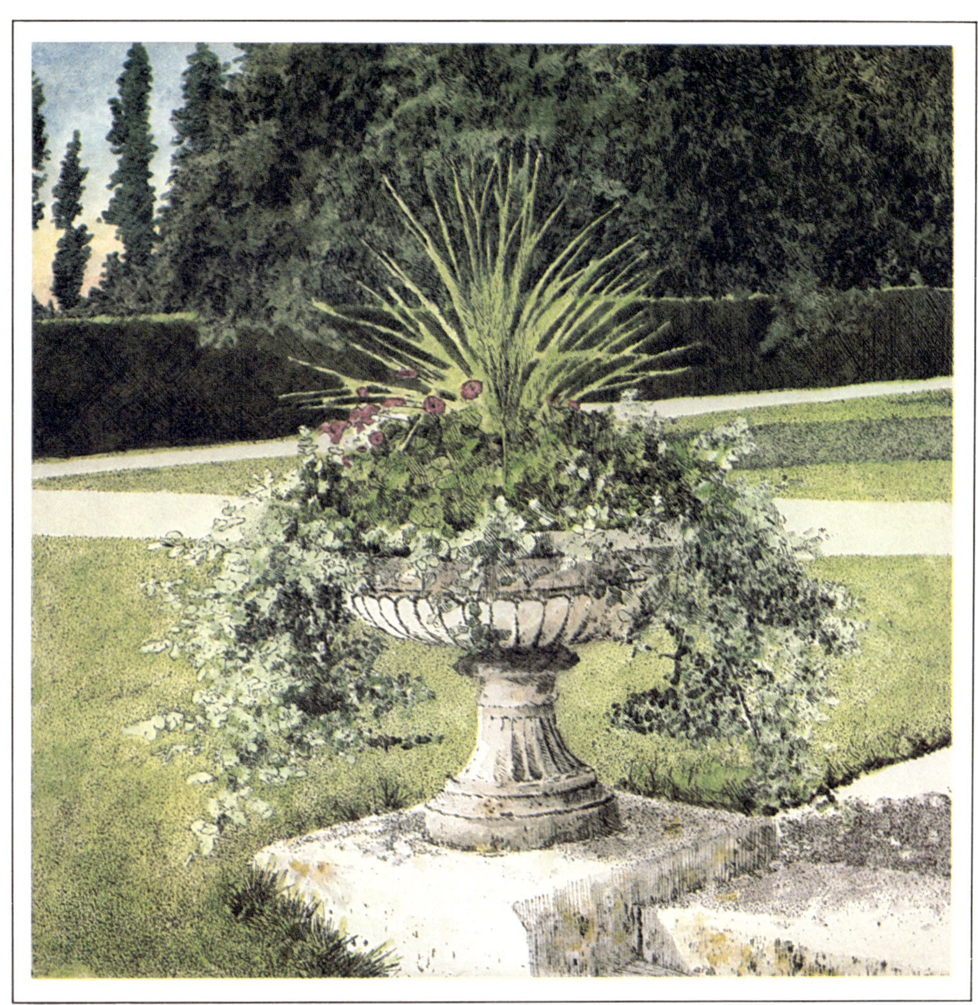

Stone Urn ~ Queen Mary's Rose Garden, Regent's Park

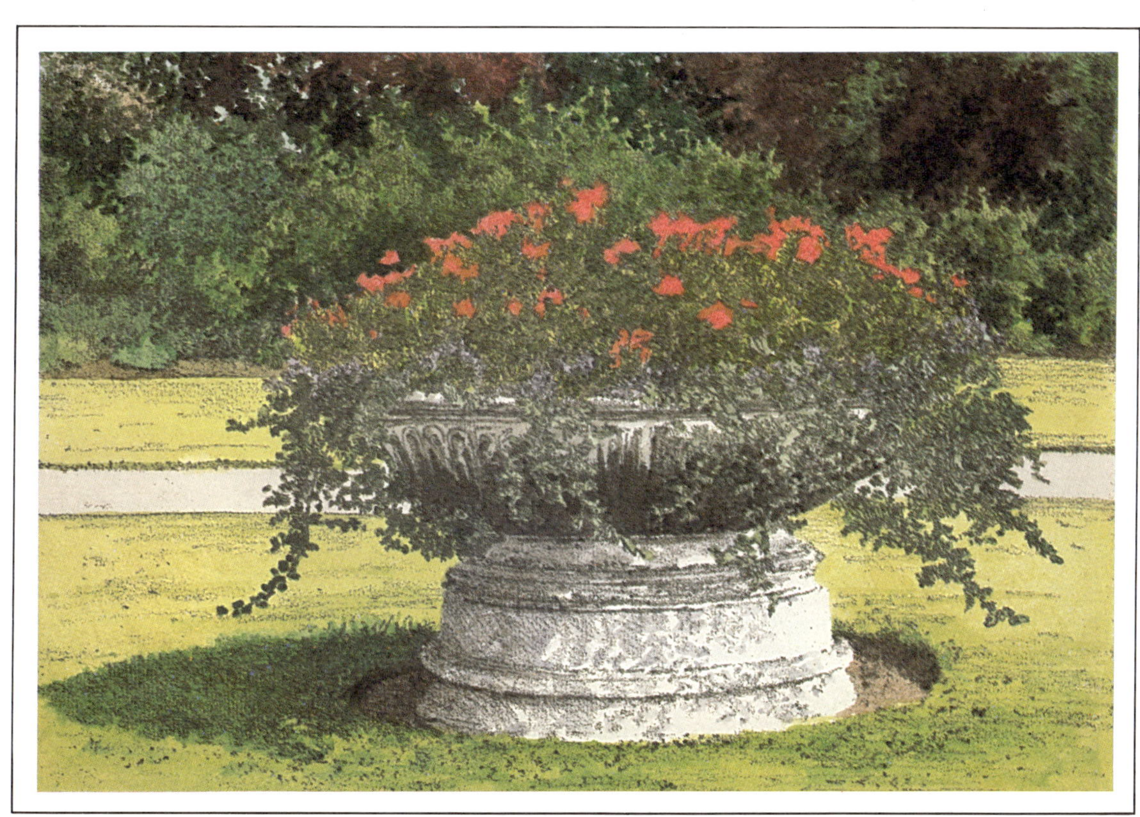

Large stone urn – Queen Mary's Rose Garden

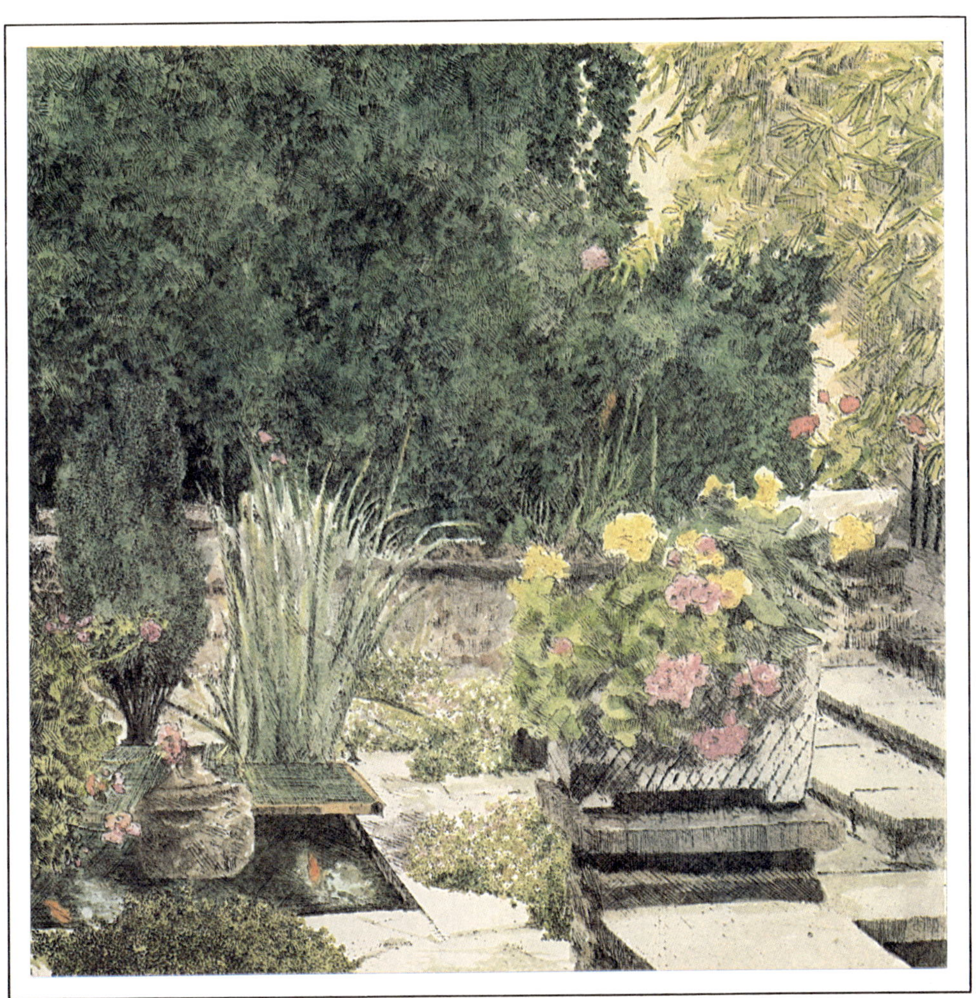

Private garden + fish pond ~ Chesterfield Hill, Mayfair

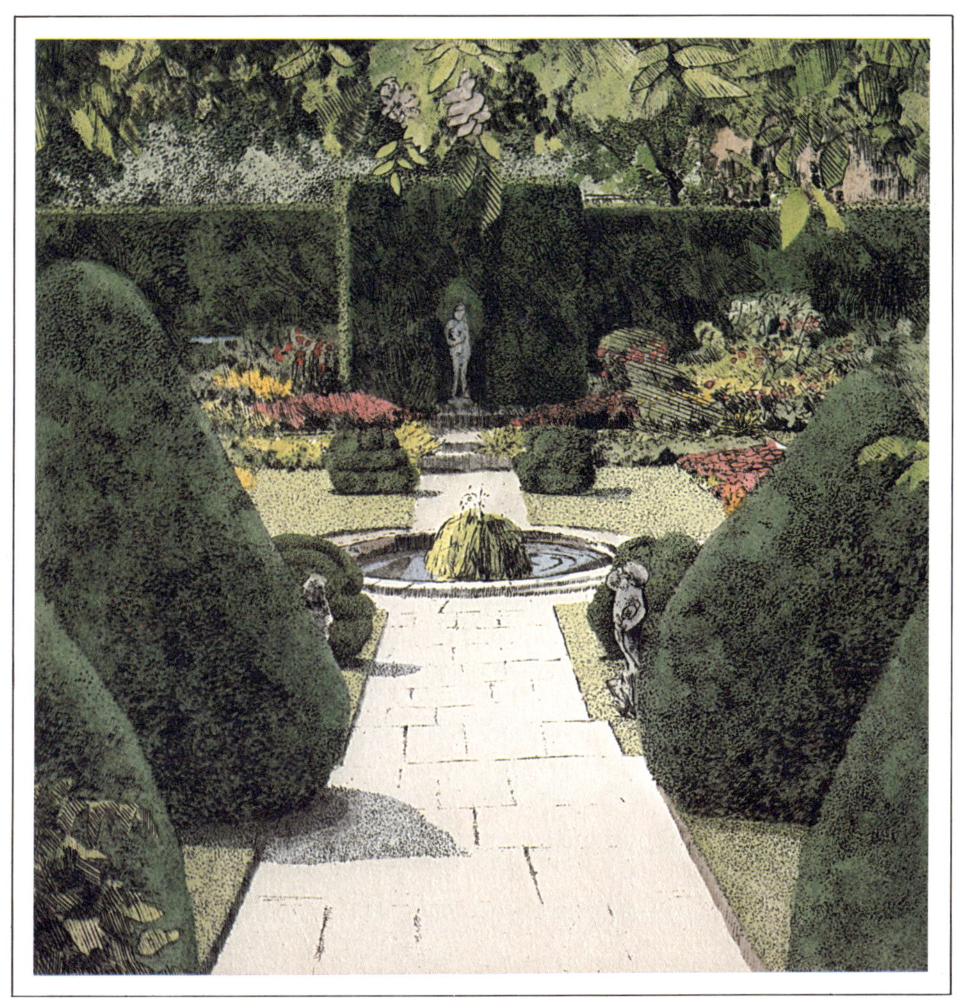

Enclosed garden ~ Hampton Court

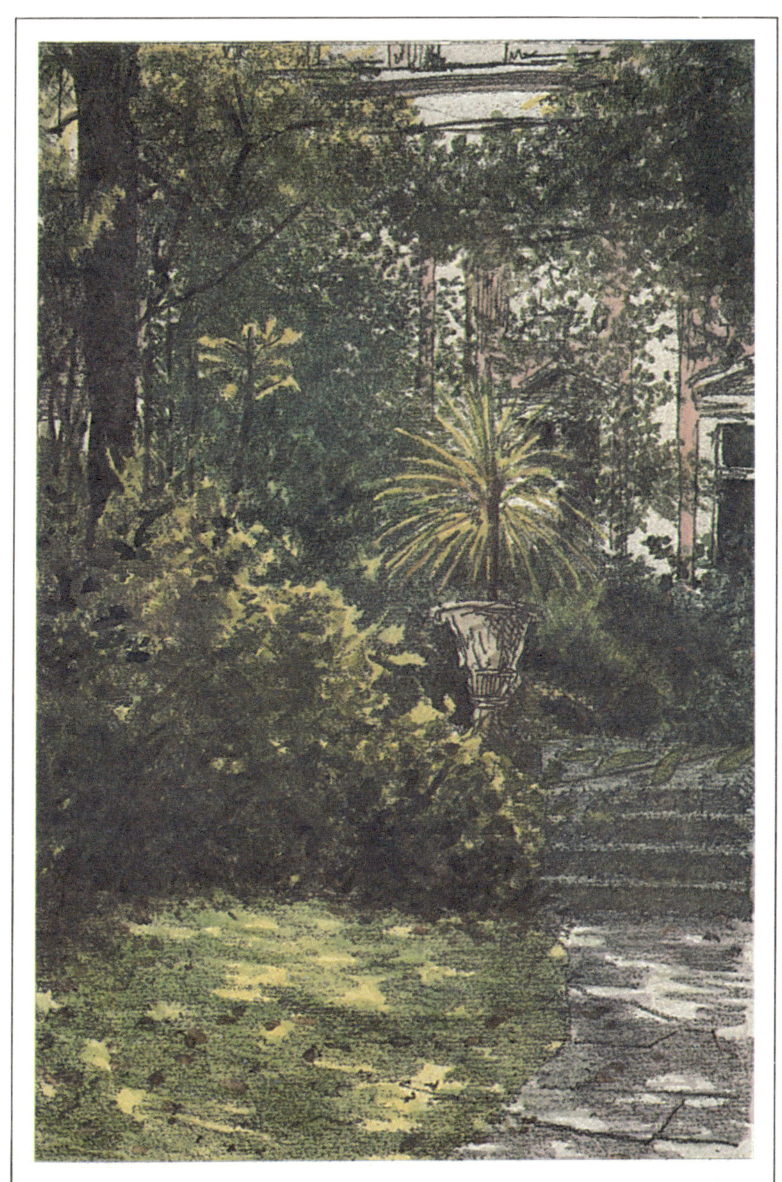

Shadowed garden ~ Gt. West Road, Notting Hill

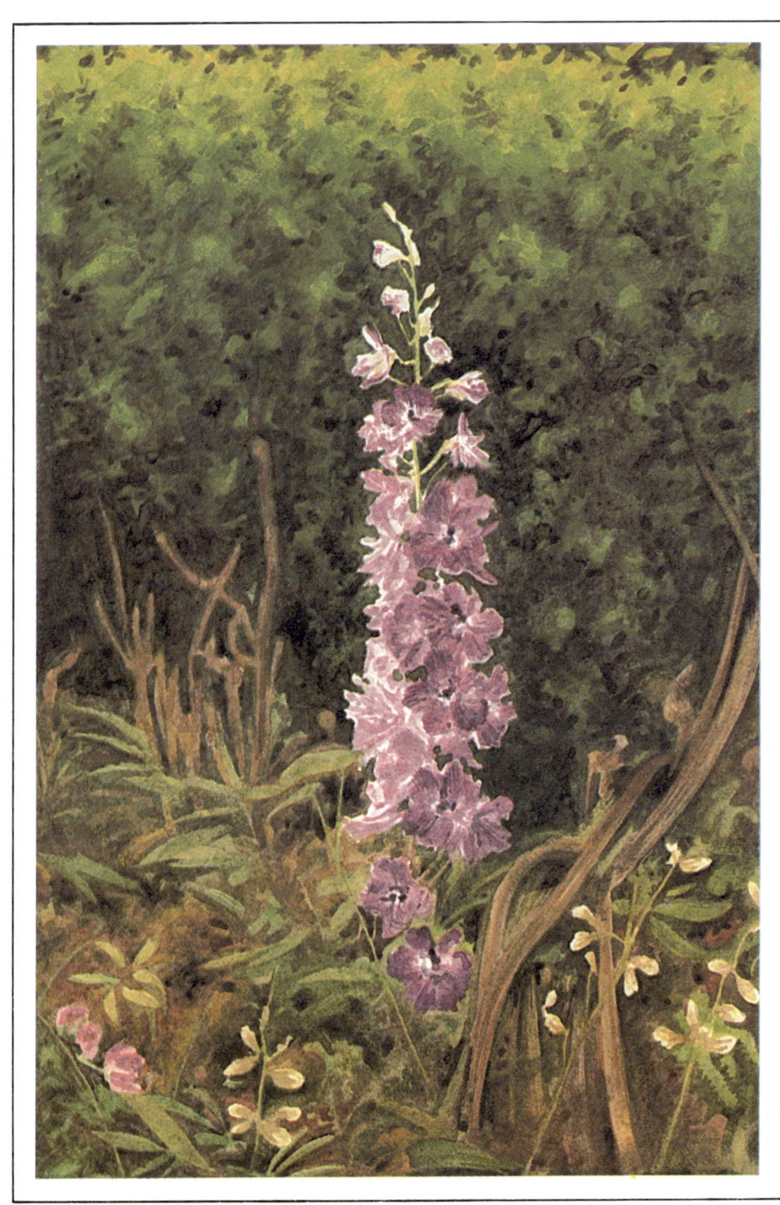

Hollyhock ~ Hampstead

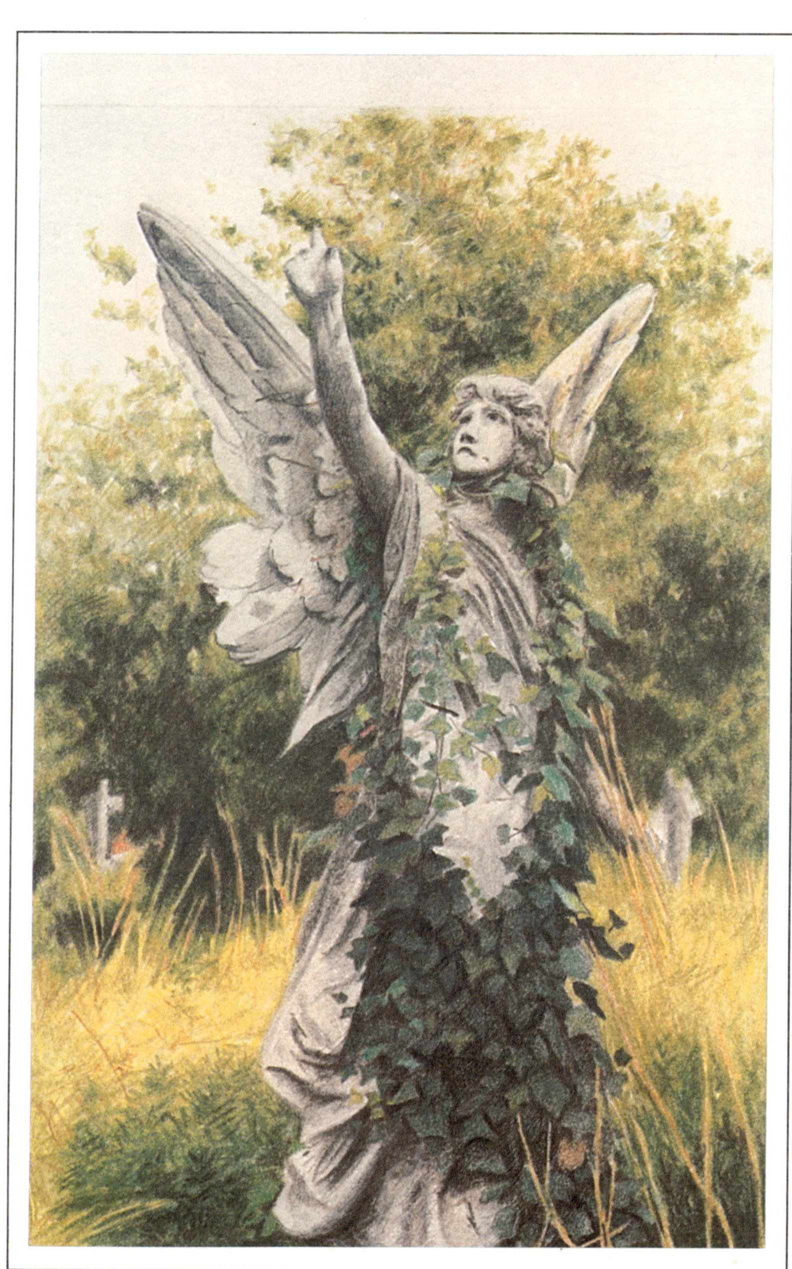

Broken-fingered angel ~ Highgate Cemetary

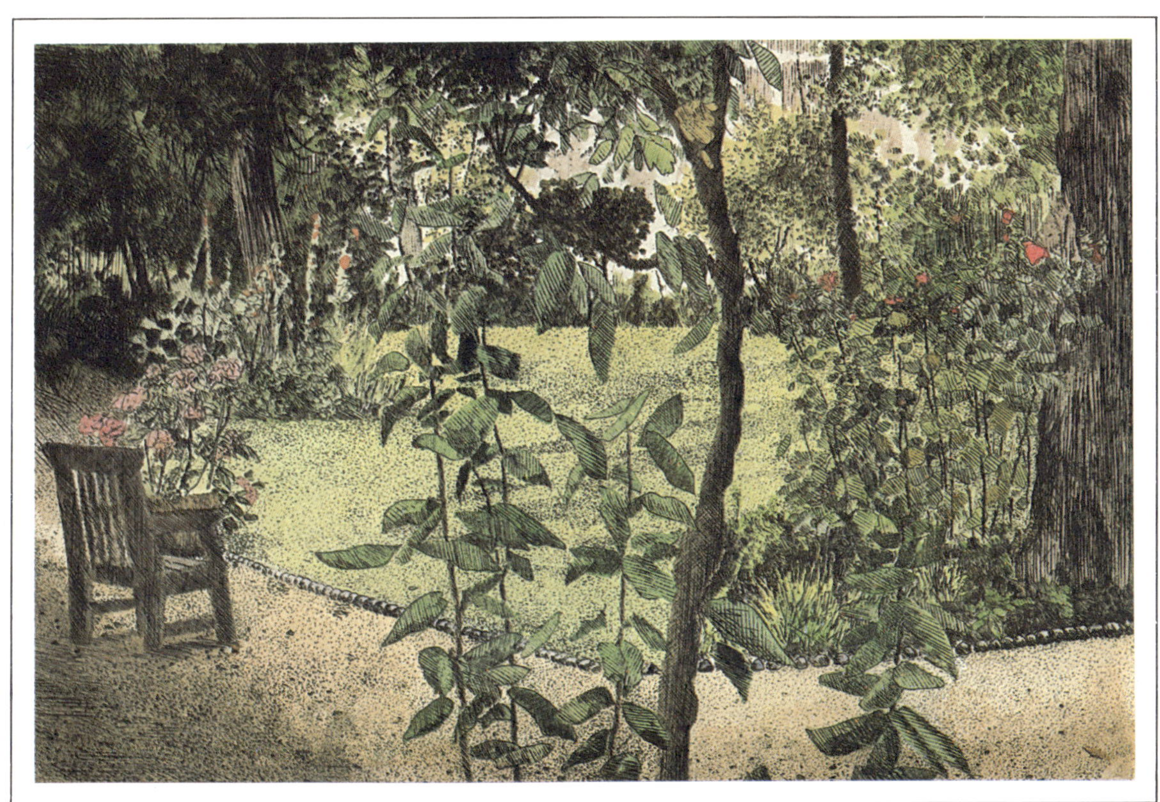

Armchair + bush screen ~ Manchester Square

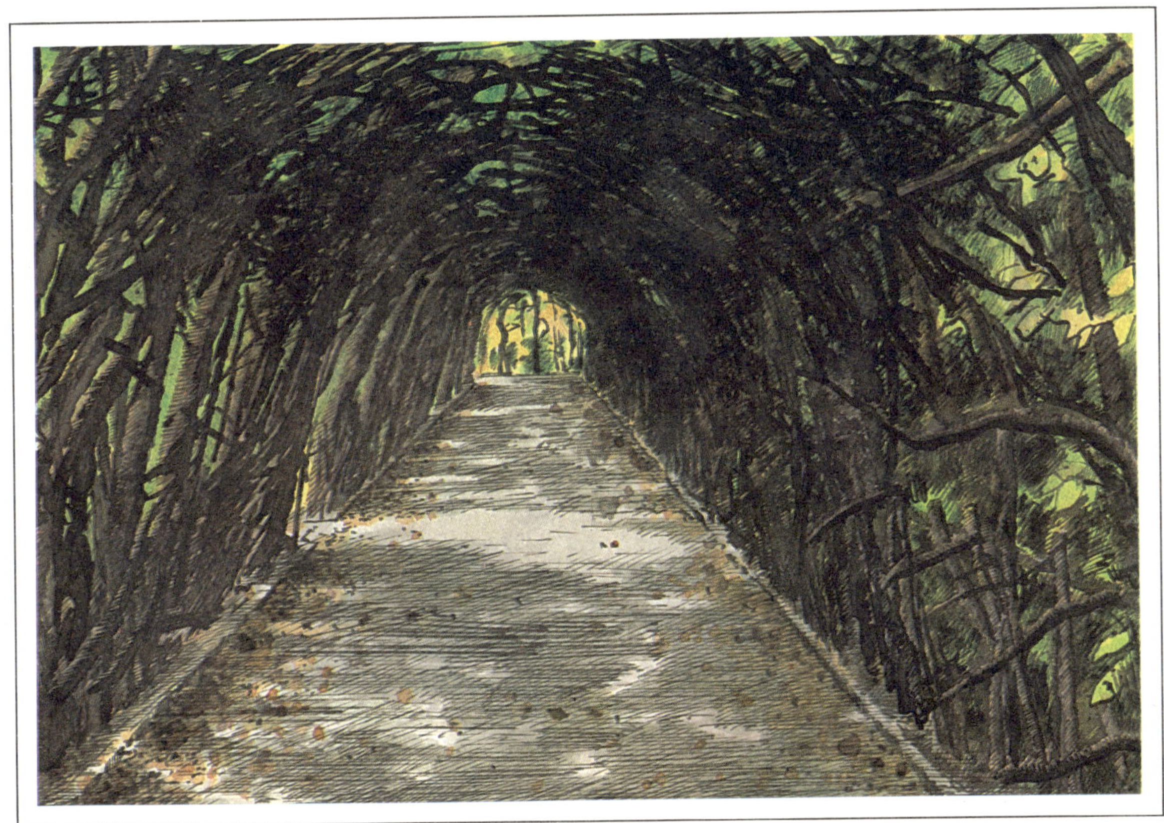

Covered Walk ~ Kensington Gardens

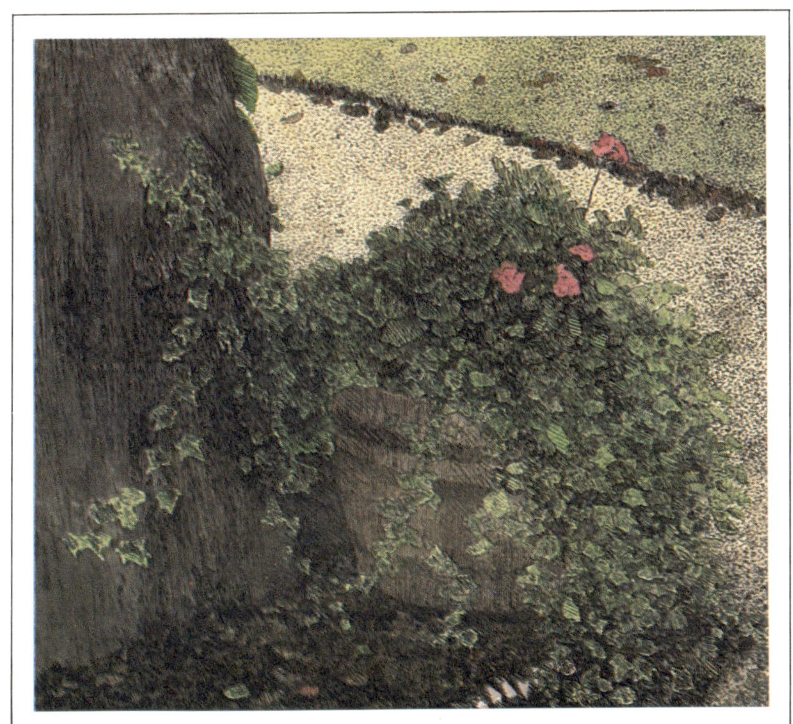

Tub of ivy ~ Kensington Square

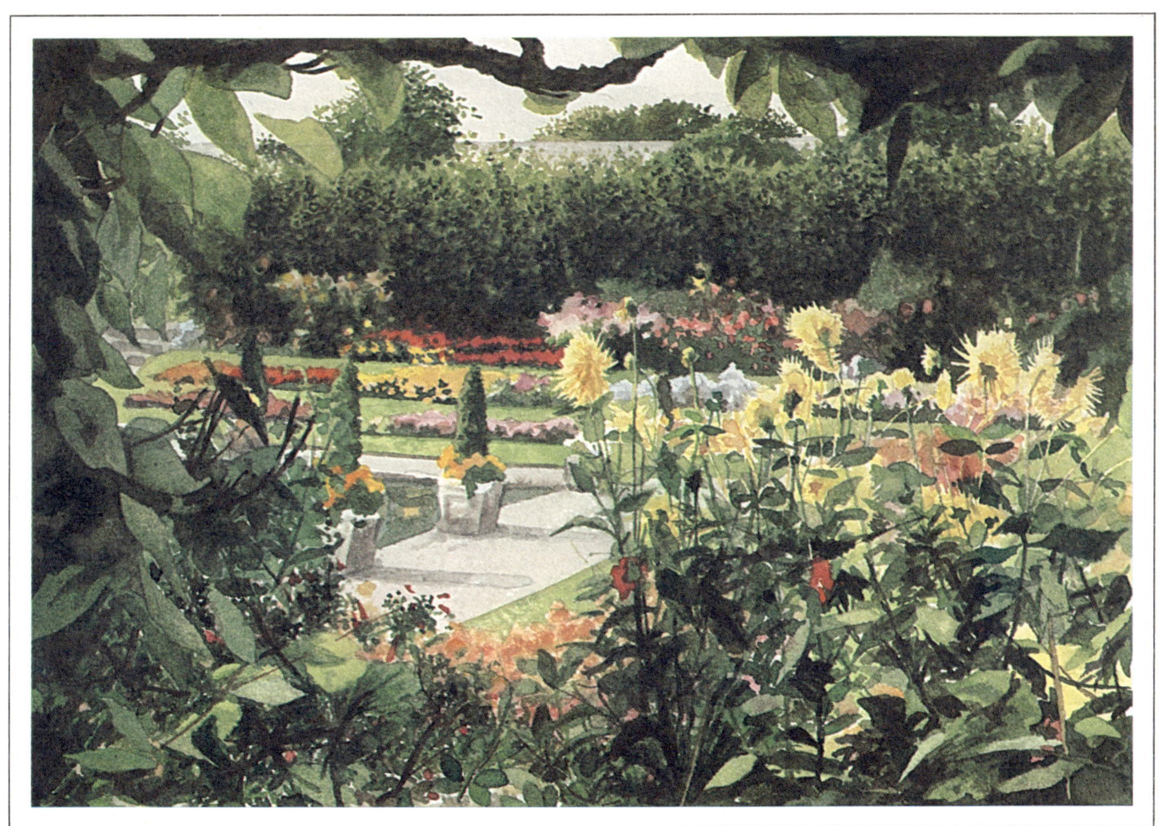

View through sunken garden ~ Kensington Palace Gardens

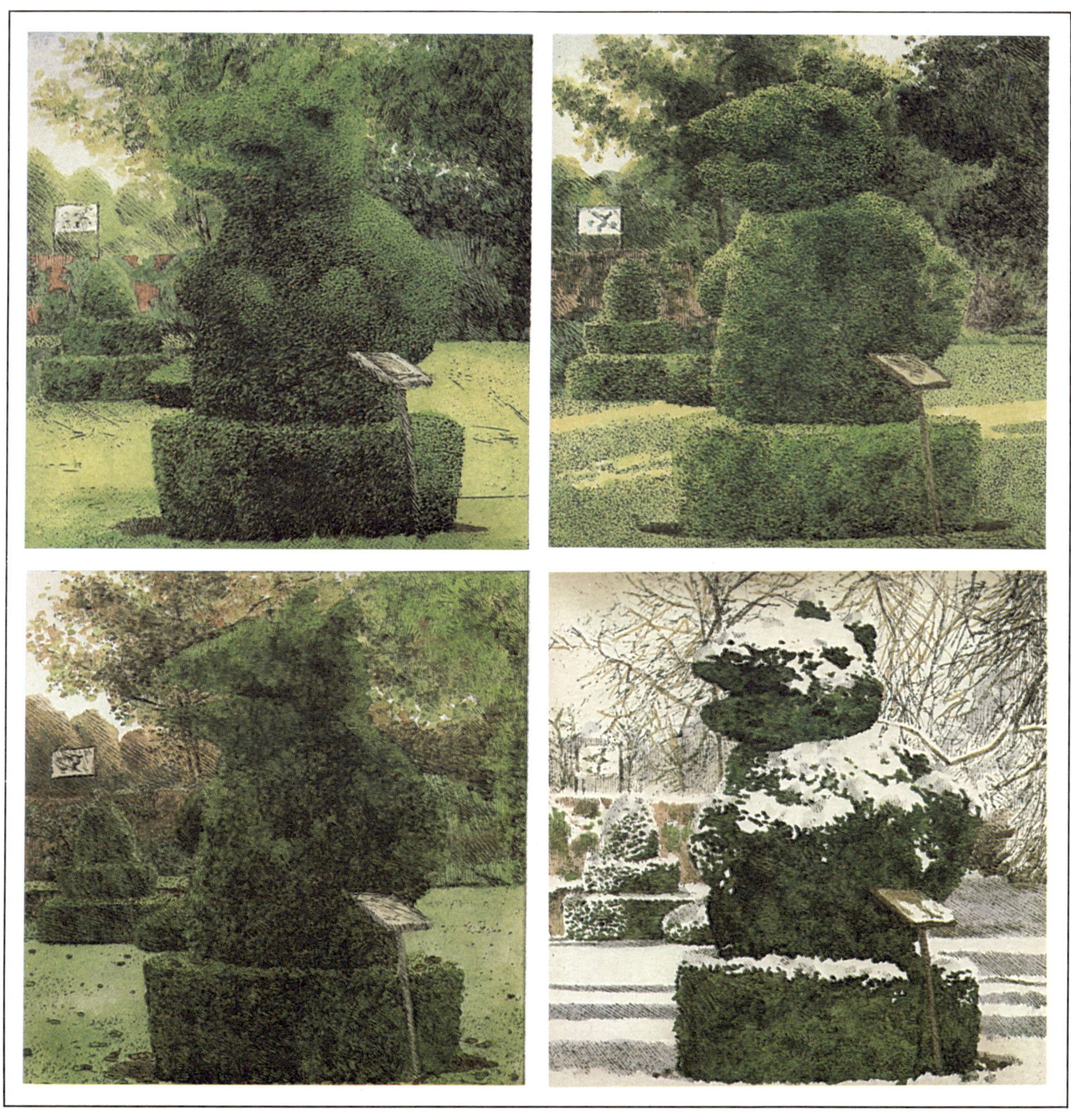

'Four Seasons' ~ The Queen's Beasts, Hall Place Gardens

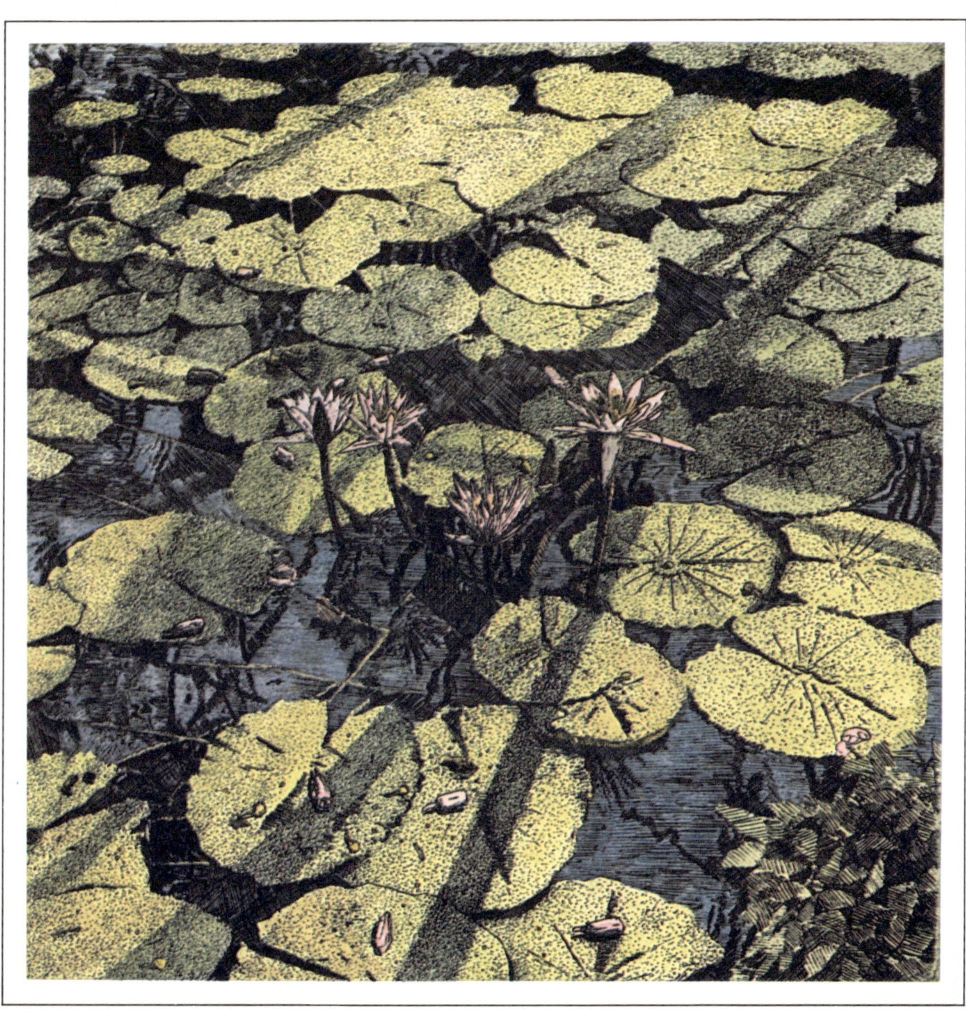

'Blue Beauty' Nymphaea ~ Lily house, Kew Gardens

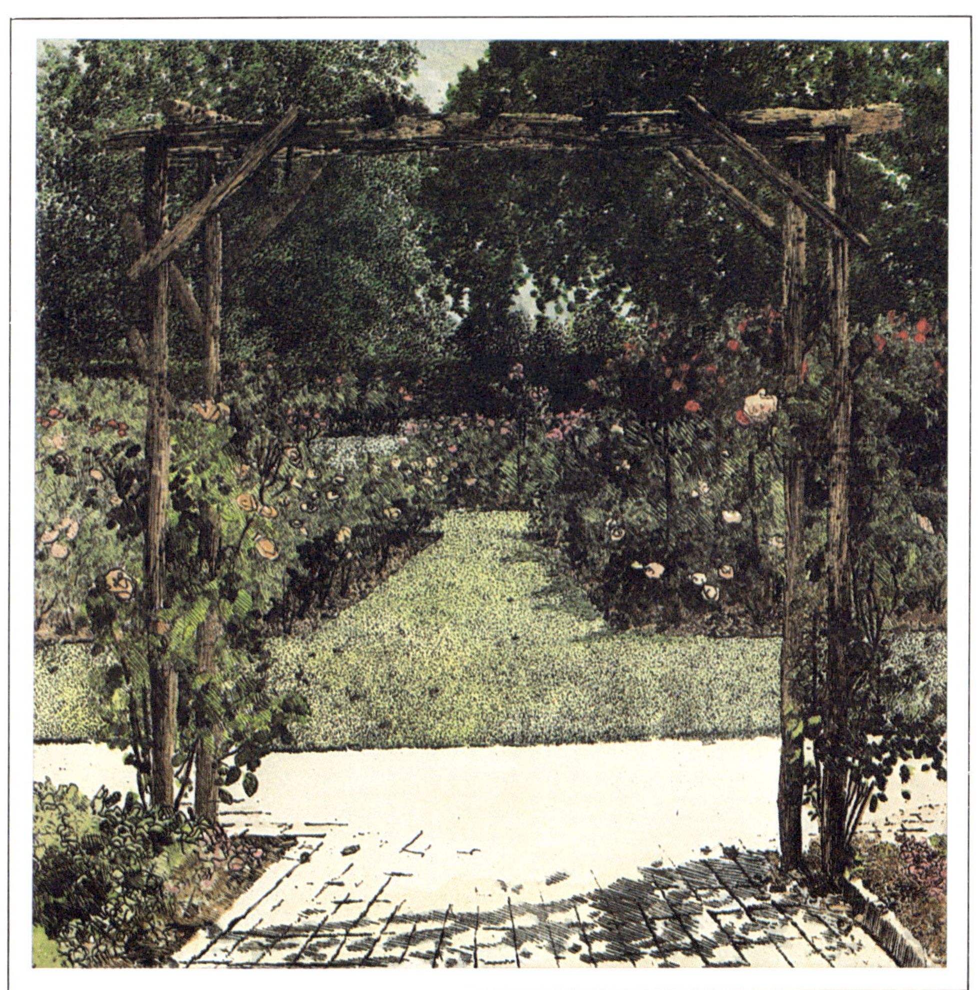

Rustic gateway ~ Hall Place Gardens, Bexley

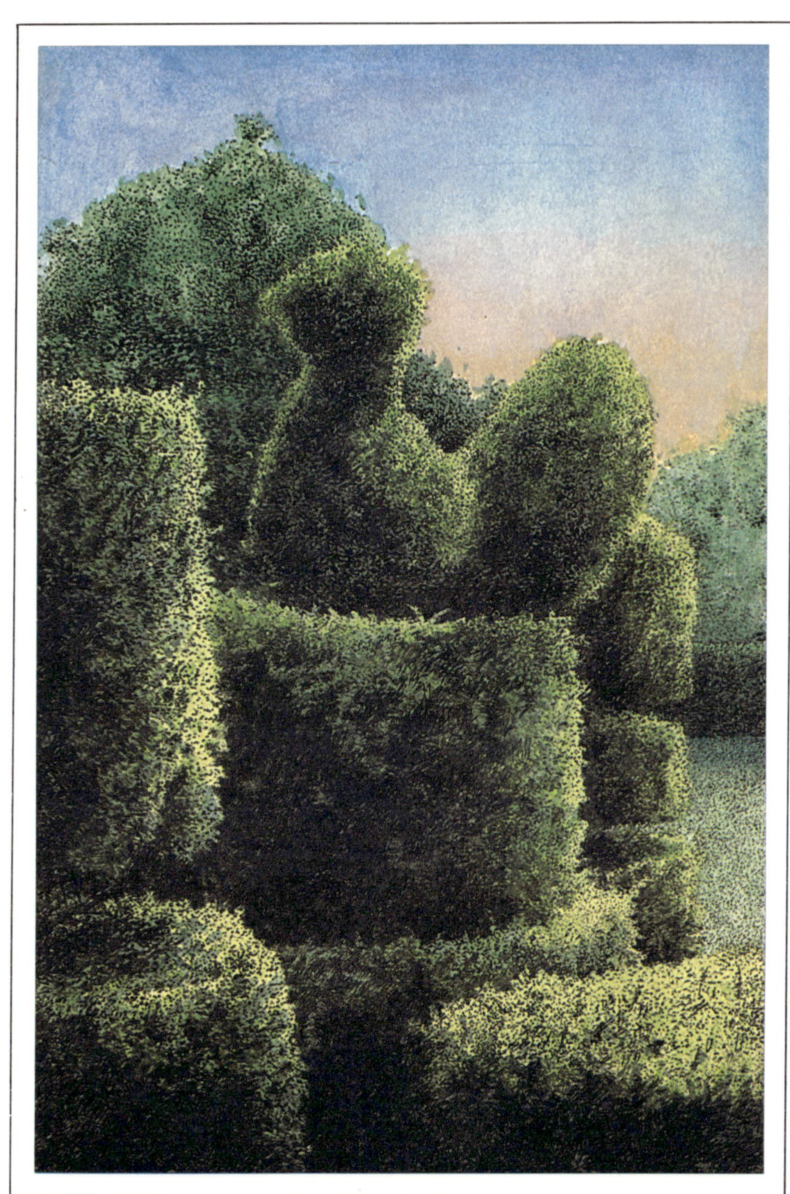

Topiary bush ~ Hall Place Gardens

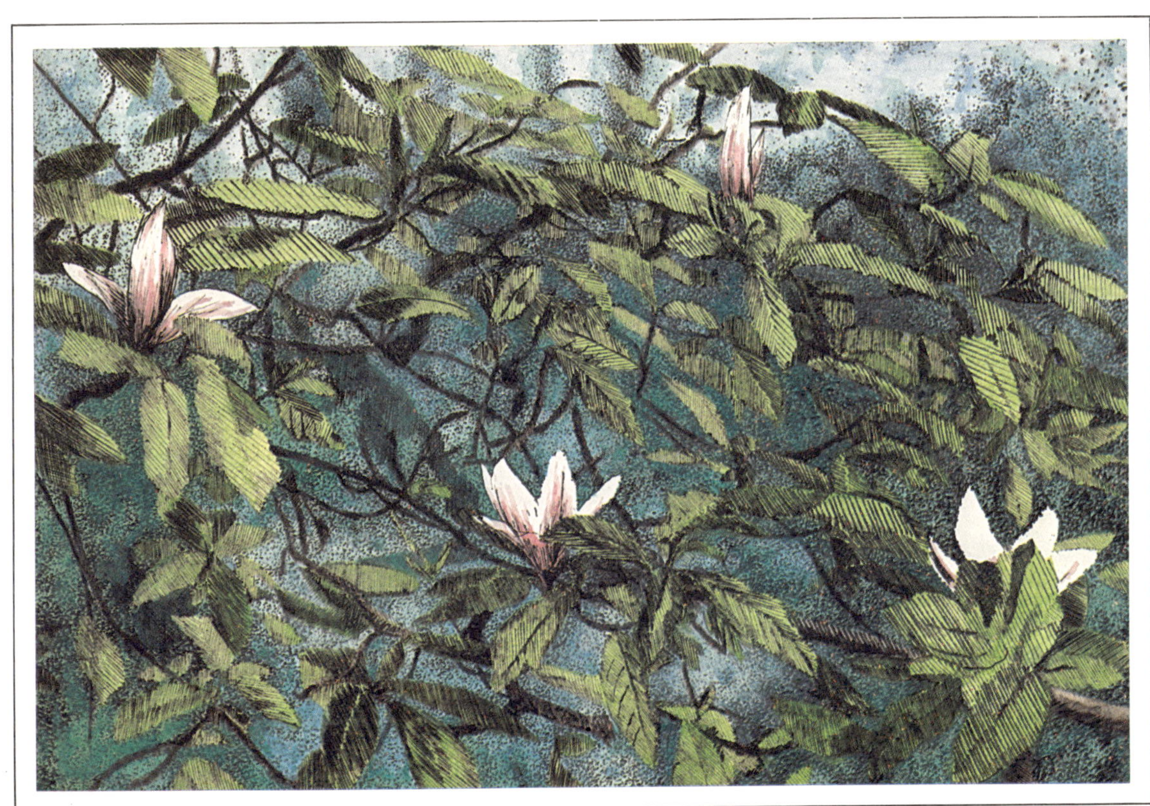

Magnolia ~ Hyde Park

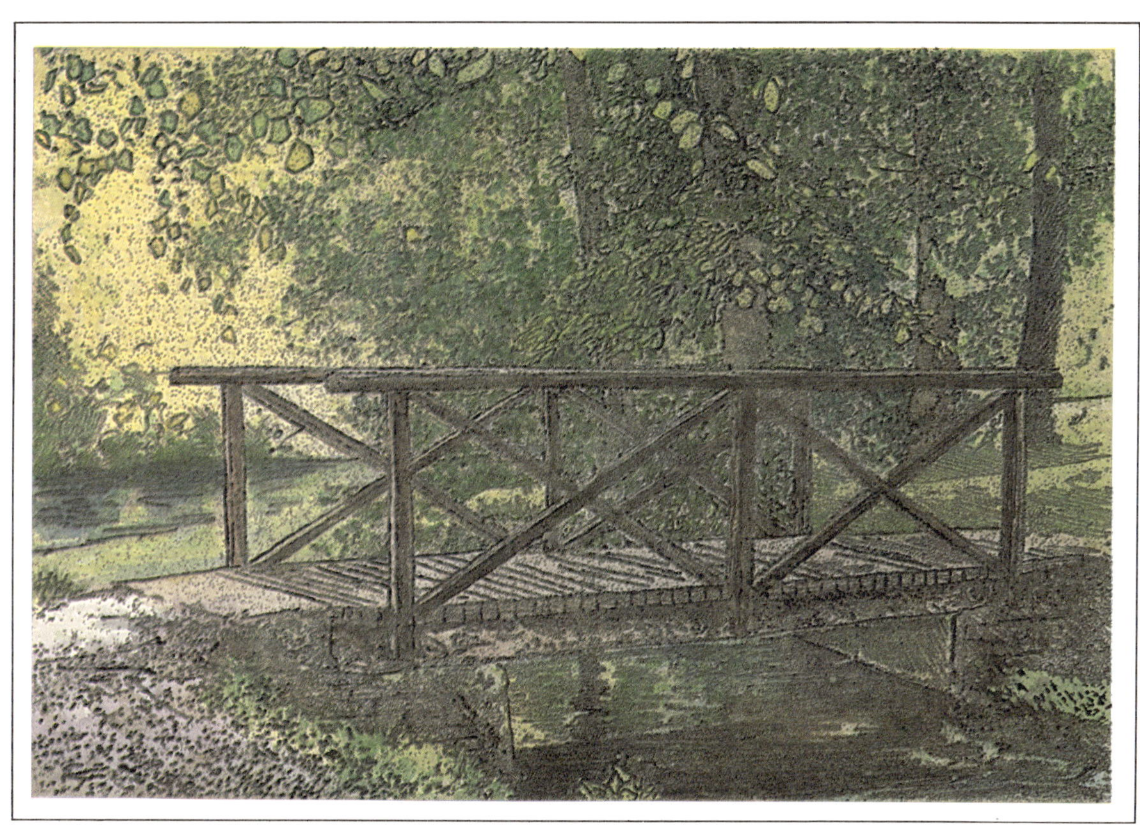

Rustic bridge ~ Bushey Park

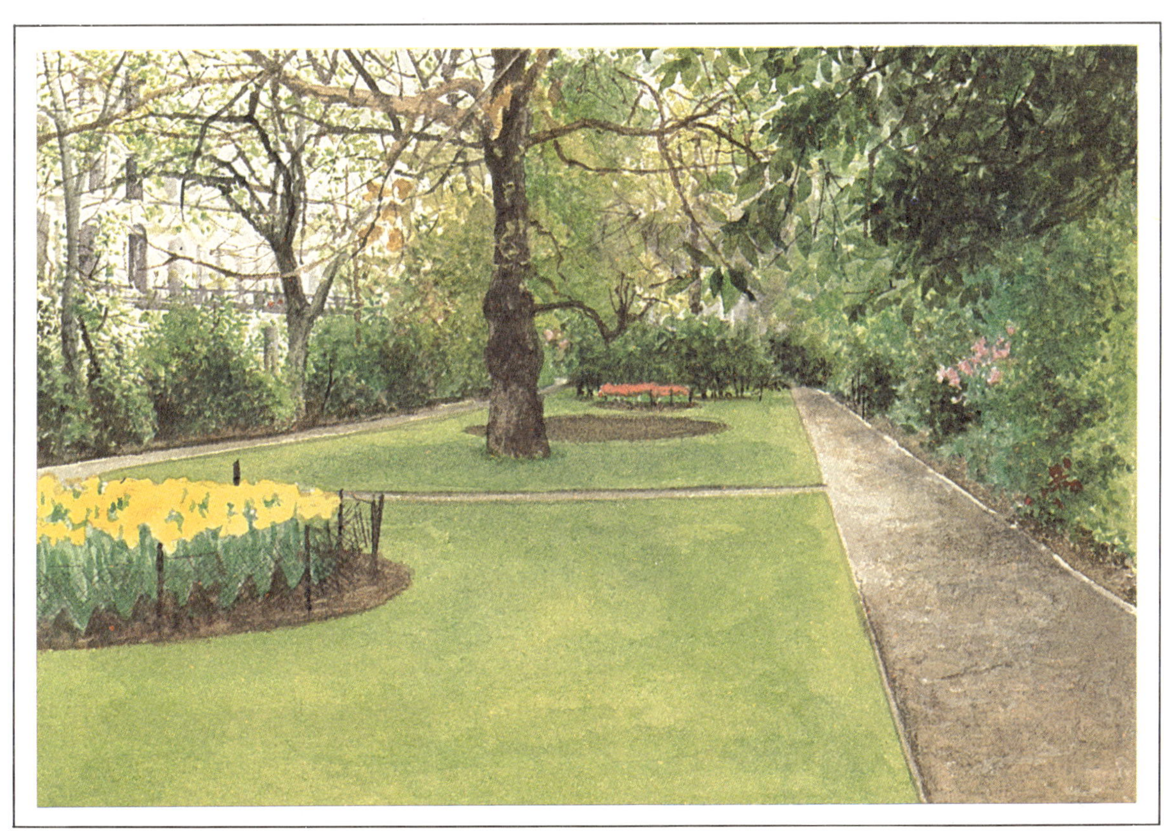

Chester Square, Belgravia

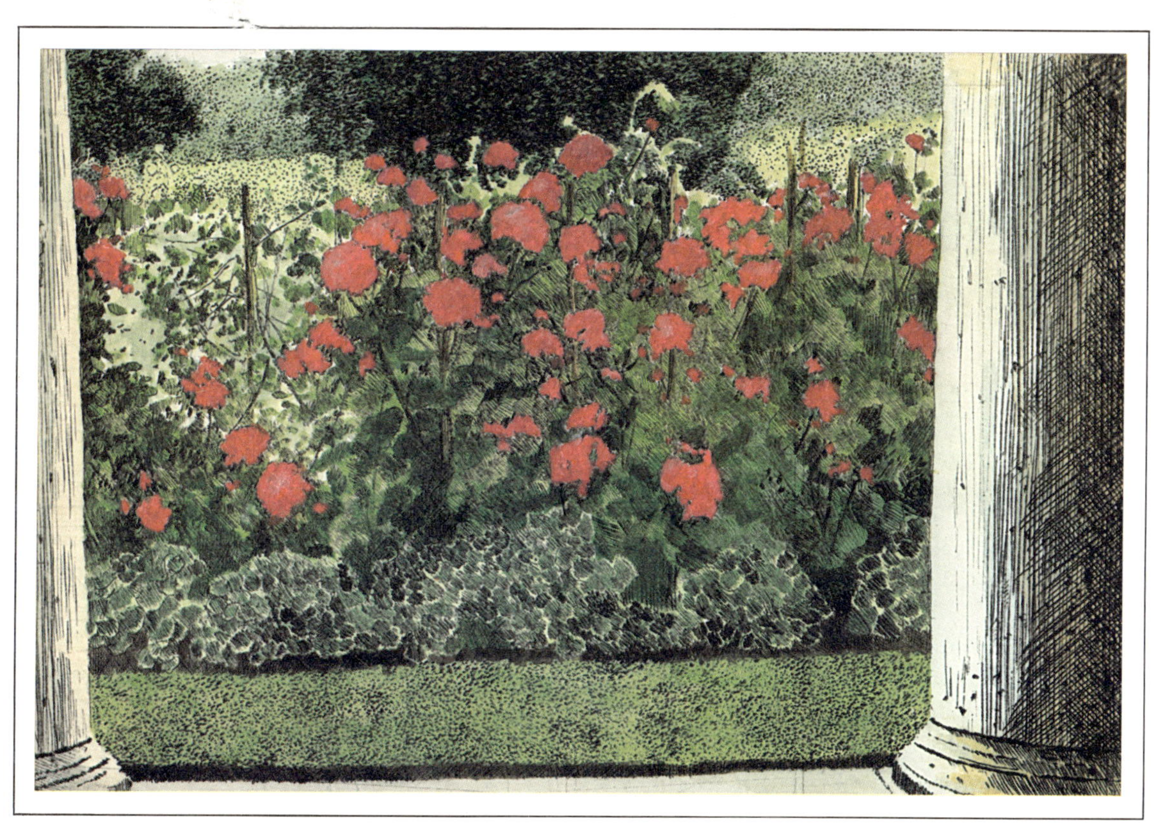

Geranium causeway ~ Royal Maritime Museum, Greenwich

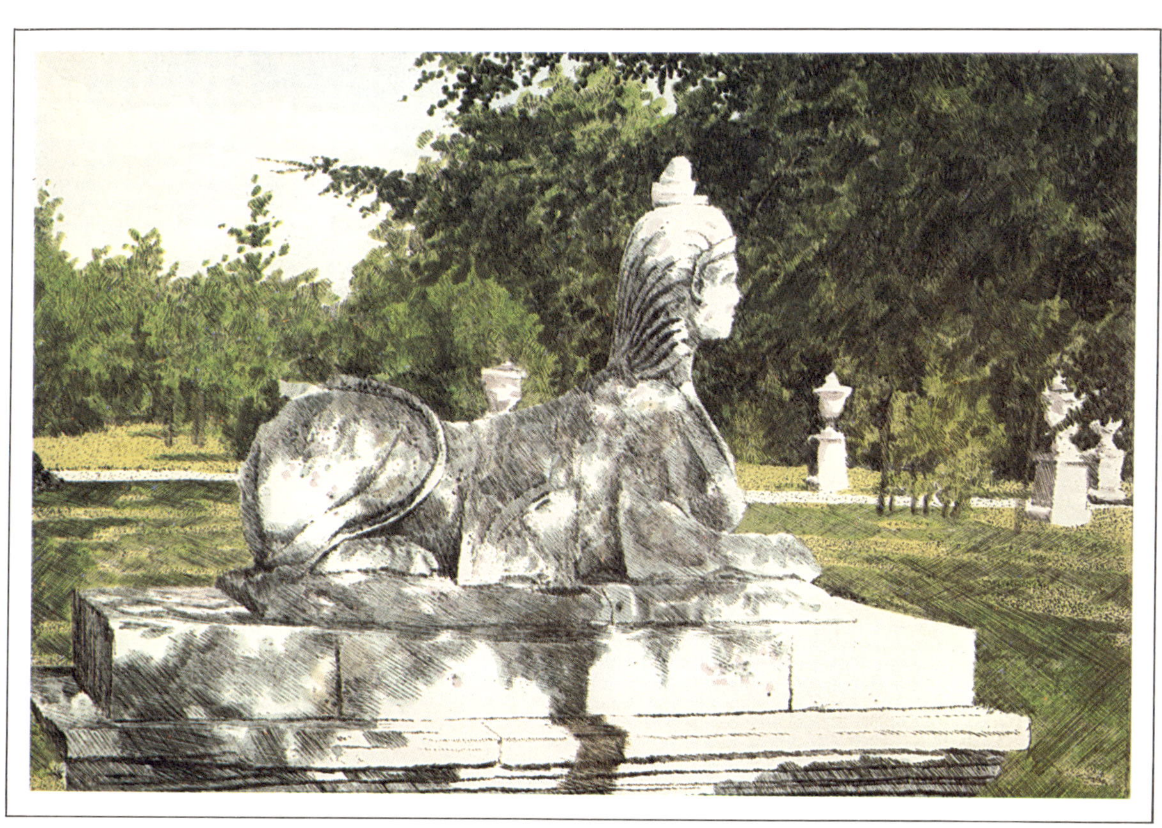

Stone Sphinx, Chiswick House